Looking at Minibeasts

Ladybirds and Beetles

Sally Morgan

Belitha Press

Contents

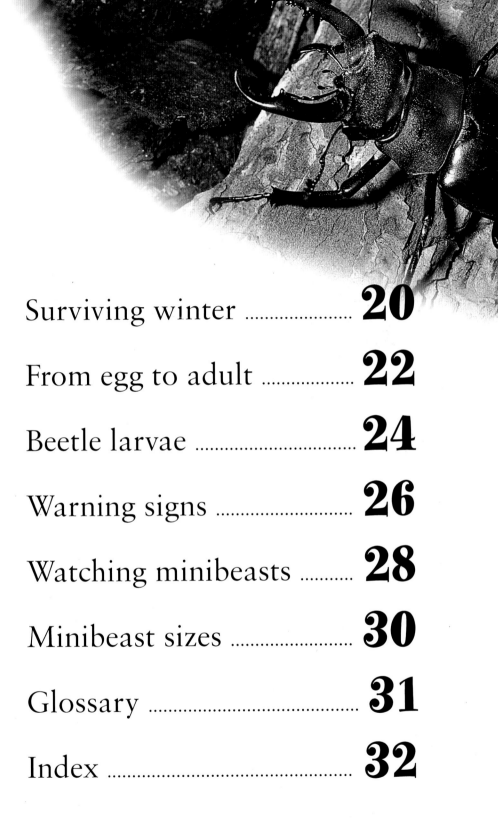

Words in **bold** are explained
in the glossary on page 31.

4

What is a ladybird?

A ladybird is a small red beetle with black spots. Beetles are part of a large group of animals called **insects**. All insects have six legs and three parts to their body. A ladybird has two big eyes and two feelers, or **antennae**, on its head. It has strong jaws to bite into food.

The beetle family

There are thousands of types of beetle.

They are many sizes, shapes and colours.

Beetles have two pairs of wings, one

hard and one soft. Most beetles live

on the ground, but some live in water.

*The hard covering of
a flower chafer beetle is
brightly coloured.*

This stag beetle uses
its horns to fight other
beetles and insects.

A water beetle has
powerful legs to help
it swim through water.

Colours and spots

Ladybirds can be different colours. Some have black spots on red or yellow wings. Other ladybirds have white spots on red wings. The number of spots varies too. Most ladybirds have seven spots. The smallest number of spots a ladybird can have is two – one on each wing. Some ladybirds have as many as 22 spots.

Flying around

A ladybird has two pairs of wings which it uses to fly. One pair of wings is stiff and red. Underneath these is a **delicate** pair of wings which are larger and thinner.

When a ladybird takes off, it opens its wings and moves them up and down. The wings carry it into the air. When a ladybird lands, it tucks its wings away in their hard case.

This cockchafer beetle is ready to fly off.

A longhorn beetle has a pair of colourful wings and a pair of delicate wings.

In the garden

A ladybird's favourite food is greenfly. Greenflies are **pests** that live on plants and suck their **sap**. A ladybird can eat as many as 50 greenflies in a day. Other beetles are helpful in the garden too. The black ground beetle likes eating snails. But some beetles are pests because they eat plants.

A ladybird uses its strong jaws to bite into greenflies.

The red lily beetle (above) is a pest because it eats garden plants.

Greenflies (left) gather on young plant shoots to suck their sap.

Hunting beetles

Some beetles are **carnivores**. This means they eat other animals. Ground beetles hunt at night. They run quickly across the ground, searching for **prey**. They like to eat slugs and snails. When they find one they use their powerful jaws to catch and hold them.

The violet ground beetle helps farmers by eating insects that damage crops.

The ground beetle
(right) has strong legs
and powerful jaws.

The tiger beetle (below)
runs very fast. It chases
small insects and catches
them in its strong jaws.

Feeding on plants

Beetles that eat plants are called **herbivores**. Many beetles feed on leaves, wood, fruit or seeds. Other beetles eat petals or drink **nectar** from flowers. When a beetle visits a flower it becomes covered with pollen. The beetle carries the pollen to other flowers. This helps the flower to make seeds.

The cardinal beetle lives in woods. It likes to sit on leaves and flowers, and under bark.

In summer, the rose chafer (above) sits on the petals of large flowers.

Weevils use their sharp jaws to suck the sap from plant stems.

Nature's dustmen

Some beetles are like insect dustmen. Dung beetles roll animal **dung** into a ball and push it into a tunnel. A female beetle lays an egg in the dung. When the egg hatches, the young beetle has plenty of food. Sexton beetles are called grave diggers. They bury dead animals.

This dung beetle is rolling a ball of dung towards a hole in the ground.

Scarab beetles feed
on the dung and dead
bodies of animals.

This sexton beetle is
sitting on the body
of a dead mouse.

Surviving winter

In winter, ladybirds need a warm, dry place to sleep through the cold weather. Their favourite places are cracks in window frames and walls. They huddle together to keep warm. Other beetles crawl under logs. When the days become longer and warmer, the beetles come out again.

Ladybirds pile up on top of each other to stay warm in winter.

These ladybirds are
sleeping in a group
on a plant stem.

Ladybirds are crawling
over this log, looking
for a place to sleep.

From egg to adult

In early summer, a female ladybird lays up to 200 eggs. Each egg hatches into a young ladybird called a **larva**. After three weeks the skin of the larva hardens. It becomes a **pupa**. Inside the pupa the larva's body changes. Soon, a new **adult** ladybird emerges from the pupa.

A new ladybird pushes out of its pupa.

Ladybirds (above) lay
their eggs on leaves,
close to greenflies.

A ladybird larva looks
like a black caterpillar
with yellow spots.

Beetle larvae

Beetle larvae hatch from eggs, just like ladybirds. A beetle larva is called a **grub**. The grub lives in the ground, feeding on the roots of plants. It may stay as a larva

A cockchafer larva has a fat white body and a brown head with powerful jaws.

for several years. Then it changes into a pupa.

An adult beetle emerges from the pupa in spring.

The female cockchafer beetle (above) lays her eggs in the summer.

An adult beetle squeezes out of its pupa in the soil.

Warning signs

The bright red colour of the ladybird is a warning. It tells other animals that it is **poisonous** to eat. If a ladybird is attacked, it rolls on to its back and squirts a smelly yellow liquid over its attacker.

The devil's coach horse beetle curls its tail to look fierce.

These ladybird larvae squeeze out blobs of smelly liquid when they are attacked.

A bloody-nosed beetle squirts a smelly red liquid from its mouth.

Watching minibeasts

In summer you can find ladybirds close to greenflies. Greenflies live on roses, willow and beans. Use a magnifying glass to count the number of spots on the ladybirds you find.

You will see beetles under stones and logs, or you can catch them in a pit fall trap. Ask a parent or teacher to help you bury a jam jar in the ground. Cover the jar with a stone to stop rain getting in. Make sure there is a small gap between the stone and the top of the jar. Check the jar for trapped beetles every morning.

Beetles, snails, spiders and centipedes can all be caught in a pit fall trap.

An old fish tank is a good place to keep beetles for a day or two.

Put any beetles you find in a fish tank. Ask someone to help you put plenty of soil and fresh leaves into the tank for the beetles. Always put the beetles back where they were caught as soon as possible.

A log pile is a good place to watch beetles and other small animals. Beetles eat the rotting wood or use the logs for shelter.

Beetles, woodlice, centipedes, spiders and snails are some of the minibeasts that live in a log pile.

Minibeast sizes

Ladybirds and beetles come in many sizes. The pictures in this book show them much bigger than they really are. Below you can see how big some of them are in real life.

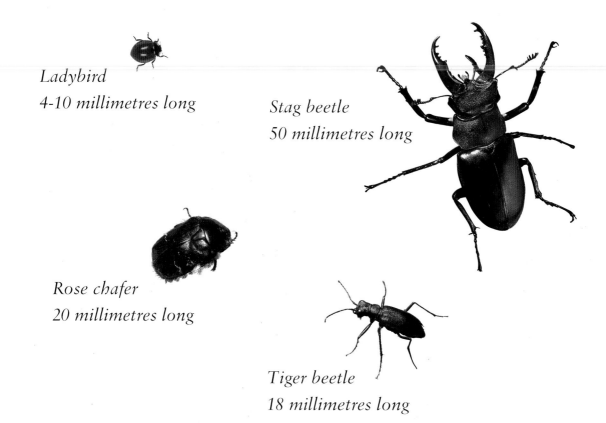

Ladybird
4-10 millimetres long

Stag beetle
50 millimetres long

Rose chafer
20 millimetres long

Tiger beetle
18 millimetres long

Glossary

adult An insect or other animal that is fully grown.

antennae The feelers on an insect's head.

carnivore An animal that eats other animals.

delicate Not strong.

dung Animal droppings.

grub A beetle larva.

herbivore An animal that only eats plants.

insect An animal with six legs and a body that is divided into three parts.

larva A young insect. It looks very different from the adult.

nectar A sugary liquid made by plants.

pest An animal that damages crops.

poisonous Harmful.

prey Animals that are killed by other animals for food.

pupa A hard case made from the skin of a larva. The larva turns into an adult inside the pupa.

sap A sweet liquid made by plants.

Index

Editor: Russell McLean
Designers: John Jamieson, Ian Butterworth
Picture researcher: Sally Morgan
Educational consultant: Emma Harvey

First published in the UK in 2000 by

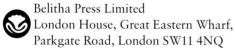
Belitha Press Limited
London House, Great Eastern Wharf,
Parkgate Road, London SW11 4NQ

Copyright © Belitha Press Limited 2000
Text copyright © Sally Morgan 2000
Illustrations by Woody

ISBN 1 84138 166 7

Printed in Singapore

British Library Cataloguing in Publication Data
for this book is available from the British Library.

10 9 8 7 6 5 4 3 2 1

Picture acknowledgements:
C. I. Bernard/OSF: 25b. Chinch Gryniewiez/Ecoscene:
13, 24. Papilio: front & back cover tr, front cover c &
b, 2t, 3, 4, 5t, 5b, 7t, 8b, 21b, 23t, 23b, 30cl, 30cr. Jean
Preston-Mafham/Premaphotos: 19b. Ken Preston-
Mafham/Premaphotos: front & back cover tcl, 2b, 6,
11c, 11br, 13t, 15b, 17t, 17b, 19t, 20, 21t, 26, 27, 30bl,
30br. Rod Preston-Mafham/Premaphotos: 15t, 27b.
Barrie Watts: front & back cover tl & tcr, 9t, 10, 12,
14, 18, 22. Robin Williams/Ecoscene: 1, 7b, 8, 16, 25t.